PowerKids Readers:

Bilingual Edition

My World of
ANIMALS™

Edición Bilingüe

BATS

MURCIÉLAGOS

NATASHYA WILSON
TRADUCCIÓN AL ESPAÑOL:
NATHALIE BEULLENS

The Rosen Publishing Group's
PowerKids Press™ & **Editorial Buenas Letras**™
New York

1

For Pete. Love you.

Published in 2004 by The Rosen Publishing Group, Inc.
29 East 21st Street, New York, NY 10010

First Edition

Book Design: Mike Donnellan
Illustration by Mike Donnellan

Photo Credits: Cover, pp. 5, 15, 17 © Merlin D. Tuttle, Bat Conservation International; p. 7 © Animals Animals/Mickey Gibson; p. 9 © Michael Durham; pp. 11, 21 © Robert and Linda Mitchell; p. 13 © Hans and Judy Beste/Animals Animals; p. 19 © Albert Visage/Peter Arnold, Inc.

Wilson, Natashya
   Bats = Murcielagos / Natashya Wilson ; translated by Nathalie Beullens.
     p. cm. — (My world of animals)
   Includes bibliographical references and index.
   Summary: This book provides an easy-to-read introduction to the life of bats and their habitat.
   ISBN 1-4042-7519-3
   1. Bats—Juvenile literature   [1. Bats 2. Spanish language materials Bilingual]   I. Title II. Title: Murcielagos   III. Series

   QL737.C5 W564 2004   2003-009077
   599.4—dc21

CONTENTS

CONTENIDO

This is a bat. Bats use their wings to fly.

Este es un murciélago. Los murciélagos utilizan sus alas para volar.

4

Bats rest upside down.
Some bats live in caves.

Los murciélagos descansan colgados cabeza abajo. Algunos murciélagos viven en cuevas.

Some bats live in trees.

Algunos murciélagos viven
en los árboles.

8

Many kinds of bats come out
at night to find food.

Muchos tipos de murciélagos
salen por la noche
a buscar comida.

Some bats eat bananas.

Algunos murciélagos
comen plátanos.

13

Some bats eat fish. They use their big claws to take the fish from the water.

Ciertos murciélagos comen peces. Usan sus garras para atraparlos en el agua.

15

Many bats eat bugs.
Bats help to keep down
the number of bugs.

Muchos murciélagos comen
insectos. Los murciélagos
ayudan a mantener bajo
control el número de insectos.

Mother bats take care of their babies. A mother bat holds her baby in her wings.

Las mamás murciélago cuidan a sus bebés. Ésta mamá murciélago sujeta a su bebé con sus alas.

19

Bats live in groups all
around the world.

Los murciélagos viven en
grupos por el mundo entero.

Words to Know
Palabras que debes saber

bananas
plátanos

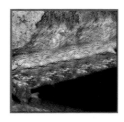

cave
cueva

claws
garras

wing
ala

Here are more books to read about bats / Otros libros que puedes leer sobre murciélagos:

In English/En inglés:
Bats and Their Homes
by Deborah Chase Gibson
Rosen Publishing

Plain-Nosed Bats
by Emily Raabe
Rosen Publishing

In Spanish/En español:
El murciélago (que está despierto)
by Patricia Whitehouse
Heinemann Library

Due to the changing nature of Internet links, PowerKids Press has developed an online list of Web sites related to the subject of this book. This site is updated regularly. Please use this link to access the list:

http://www.buenasletraslinks.com/myanim/bat

23

Index

Índice

Words in English: 92   Palabras en español: 96

Note to Parents, Teachers, and Librarians

PowerKids Readers books *en español* are specially designed for emergent Hispanic readers and students learning Spanish in the United States. Simple stories and concepts are paired with photographs of real kids in real-life situations. Sentences are short and simple, employing a basic vocabulary of sight words, as well as new words that describe familiar things and places. With their engaging stories and vivid photo-illustrations, PowerKids *en español* gives children the opportunity to develop a love of reading and learning that they will carry with them throughout their lives.